Children's Sermc

Friends and Followers
in the
Bible II

Leanne Hensley Ciampa

ABINGDON PRESS
Nashville

FRIENDS AND FOLLOWERS IN THE BIBLE II

Copyright © 1993 by Abingdon Press

This book is printed on recycled, acid-free paper.

Library of Congress Cataloging-in-Publication Data

Ciampa, Leanne Hensley, 1961–
Friends and followers in the Bible.

    (Children's sermon exchange)
    Includes index.
    1. Bible—Biography—Sermons. 2. Bible—Children's sermons. I. Sermons, American. II. Title
BS571.5C53 1991   252'.53   91-7584
ISBN 0-687-13500-1

Cover art: Doug Jones
© 1992 by Cokesbury (The United Methodist Publishing House, Nashville, TN) Used by permission.

Scripture quotations are from the New Revised Standard Version Bible, copyright © 1989, by the Division of Christian Education of the National Council of Churches of Christ in the United States of America. Reprinted by permission.

MANUFACTURED IN THE UNITED STATES OF AMERICA

To my sons,
Julian and Britton,
who remind me of how much children love to hear
Bible stories and of how much of the word of God
children can understand!

Contents

Section Four: David, a Very Good King

Section Five: Joshua, a Warrior for God

Introduction

I was born during the same year that my father graduated from seminary and was ordained a United Methodist minister. So most of my earliest memories occurred in the church where my father was pastor. I loved the church and everything about it. When the church was empty, my brothers and sisters and I would play in the sanctuary, pretending to be ministers and part of the congregation. We would play hide and seek in the various Sunday school rooms, and run races in the empty fellowship hall. An empty church was a great place to spend time, but I must admit that my favorite time of week was when that empty building became a "church" and the people gathered for worship and Sunday school.

Week after week I sat in worship and attended Sunday school. I listened and I learned and I felt loved. Being the minister's child or as many people called me, the "preacher's kid," I usually knew more answers than anyone else in my Sunday school class, and I knew the words to the doxology and Lord's Prayer long before any of the other children my age. So I grew up believing I knew a lot about church, God, and the Bible.

And I did know a lot. The church was a loving place where anyone could go and be made to feel a part of the family of God. It was a place where people worshiped and sang and gave money to help those who were less fortunate. I knew a lot about God as well. I knew that God created the world and loved me and sent God's son to be my savior. I knew God and prayed to God and knew that God loved me. I also knew a lot about the Bible. I knew all about Jesus—where he was born, the stories he told, the people he healed, his suffering and death and the resurrection.

It wasn't until much later in my life that I realized that I

7

didn't know as much about the Bible as I thought I did. I did learn a great deal about the New Testament, thanks to my wonderful Sunday school teachers. I was familiar with the life of Christ, but I was not familiar with the people who lived before him. I did not know about people of faith and courage and hope like Isaac and Jacob and Esau and Hannah and Ruth and Naomi and Joshua. Somehow in my time as a child growing up these characters were not graven in my memory. I must have learned of them at some point, but it did not stick with me. Perhaps the stories of these characters were not repeated over and over like the stories of Jesus were.

While in seminary I became fascinated with the characters of the Old Testament and the more I studied them the more fascinated I became with their stories of faith and courage and trust in God. As I faced my own trials and hard times, these people became visions of hope for me and I felt they were companions on my journey of faith.

Many times I have wondered why the stories of these people did not stick with me as a child, and as I speak to groups of adults I often ask them to jot down the names of Old Testament characters they remember. I have found that I was not the only child who missed learning about these characters. Most of the adults I have spoken to can only recall the names of five or six characters from the Old Testament, and then when asked to tell me about the characters they listed, they know even less.

For this book of children's sermons, then, I chose only Old Testament characters. Instead of well-known characters like Noah and Jonah, whom I feel most children already know, I chose less famous biblical characters whose lives reveal much about struggling to be people of God. I think that while it is appropriate for much of our worship to center around New Testament stories and the life of Christ, our children will miss many valuable lessons about faith and courage if we neglect to tell the stories of the people of the Old Testament.

I have used a variety of styles and senses to help the children not only *hear* the story but *remember* it. Most of the sermons actively involve the children in the hope that by being directly involved they will remember the stories better. I am sure you have heard it before, but it bears repeating—children remember 10 percent of what they hear and 90 percent of what they do. I must caution that when asking children to move around during a children's sermon and to respond openly and freely, we also risk the chance that the sermon will not go exactly as planned. It might seem simpler and easier to have the children sit and listen to the story. But our goal is not to be simple or to do the children's sermon as easily as possible. I believe our goal as the presenter of the children's sermon is to make the word of God come alive by presenting it in ways that the children will actively learn and remember.

I have used the New Revised Standard Version of the Bible as a basis when quoting scripture directly. However, in order to make the stories easier for children to understand, I have taken the liberty (in some of the sermons) of paraphrasing the scripture or simplifying it. I have tried, though, to remain as faithful as possible to the original translation and not to change meanings as I paraphrased.

I strongly believe that if the word of God is presented in a clear manner that captures the children's attention, they will understand the main message of the story. However, some things can be confusing for the children. First, the stories in this book are all based on Old Testament characters. The children might wonder when these people lived. For example, they are probably more familiar with Jesus and the disciples and even Paul than many of these characters. They may wonder if these people lived at the time of Jesus or if they were friends of Jesus. So it might be helpful to set a time reference for the children by explaining to them that a particular character lived a long time before Jesus was ever born.

Another confusing part of these stories might be that the people of the Old Testament had traditions and customs that were very different from our customs. For example, Jacob married two wives. You might want to begin a sermon where a very different custom is talked about by saying, "You know, this story happened a long time ago and the people who lived then did some things very differently from what we do today. For example, the man in this story, Jacob, had two wives at the same time. That seems strange to us now, but it was the custom when this story happened." It is important to point out the differences but not to dwell on them. Children usually accept statements like this without much questioning and remember, children have short attention spans. You do not want to use up their attention talking about secondary issues and then not have their total attention during the sermon.

These sermons are intended to be used in a worship setting; however, I encourage their use wherever lessons about the Old Testament characters are being studied. Children's choir, vacation Bible school, children's church and Sunday school are excellent places where these sermons can supplement the lesson being taught. Many Christian preschools and day care centers use sermons such as these as a part of their opening moments for the day. Some private in-home care givers of children use the sermons to teach the children whom they care for. So while these sermons are written in the context of worship, I encourage you to be creative and have fun discovering new situations where children can experience the word of God. Their brevity make them good for a variety of settings.

The book is arranged so that each entry contains the scripture reference for the sermon, a brief summary of the story being told, the learning objectives, and the materials needed. The sermon is written out, followed by a prayer which often summarizes once more what the story has to say to children about faith and God. At the end of each section are suggestions for delivery. I actually give the children's sermon at my church, and so the sermons in the book have been tested with groups of children. Each time I give a sermon I try to identify what part of the delivery can enhance or detract from the sermon and then write about it in the suggestions for delivery. I hope that they are helpful and that they help you avoid some problems in the sermon. At the end of the book is a Scripture index which will assist you in finding the specific text you wish to use.

These sermons were developed so that they can be used individually, but they are written so that they can also be used as a logical series. You may choose to use an isolated sermon as the text is appropriate or you may choose to teach an entire section on consecutive Sundays. If you choose to teach an entire section, it would be best to briefly review what the children learned about the character the week before.

"Making the word of God come alive" sounds like such an overwhelming and difficult task. I do think it is an important ministry. I have a vision of children who experience the word of God and then grow into people of faith as adults because they are able to remember and identify with these faith-filled people. We are fortunate to share the stories with children and watch their enthusiasm and excitement about the word of God. So I hope you take the task as seriously as I do, but at the same time, I hope you relax and enjoy the spontaneity and joy which the children show in response. This is important and challenging work—but what joy we will receive in return.

May God bless you and also bless all the children whose lives you touch!

11

Jacob, a Man Who Learned to Follow God

Two Jealous Brothers

Scriptural Base: *Genesis 25:19-27*

Scriptural Summary

Isaac, the son of Abraham, appeals to God to give his wife Rebekah a child. His prayers are answered and she becomes pregnant with twins. The babies fight while still in the womb. When Rebekah asks God about it, she is told that the children will each found a nation and will fight from the day of their birth. She is also told that the second born child will be stronger than the first. The prophecy comes true; the brothers fight constantly. Esau, the eldest, becomes a hunter and Jacob, the younger brother, becomes a tent dweller.

Learning Objectives

To truly understand the motivations and the spiritual changes Jacob goes through as he grows from a boy to a man of God, it is important that the children learn about and understand the relationship he and his older brother had. This sermon attempts to explain that relationship.

It also addresses the issue of sibling rivalry which all children who have siblings experience in one form or another. Many children feel a need to constantly outdo their siblings in order to win the attention, approval, or even love of a parent. This sermon addresses sibling rivalry as a normal emotion.

Materials Needed

Two sheets of poster board numbered from one to five and a marker.

The Sermon

Today I want to tell you a story about two brothers. Do any of you have a brother or sister? (Let the children respond by raising hands.) Are any of you a twin? (Let them respond.) Do you know what a twin is? (They will most likely respond with things like "two people born at the same time" and "they look alike.") The story I want to tell you is about two brothers who were also twins. And do you know that they started to fight before they were ever born? Then, after they were born they always tried to outdo each other and prove that they were the best. I want to show you what it was like to be around them.

One brother, the older one, was named Esau. Could one of you stand up here and pretend to be Esau? (Choose a child.) The other brother was named Jacob. Would one of you pretend to be Jacob? (Choose a second child and stand them facing the children side by side. Give each child one poster board numbered 1-5.) Now these two don't look alike do they? Some twins look alike, but not Jacob and Esau, they were very different. Now we are going to list the different qualities of these two twins. We will start with Esau. Esau had very red hair all over his body. (Write "red hair" on that sheet.) We aren't told what color hair Jacob had, but let's say it was brown. (Write "brown hair" on the other sheet.) Esau was a hunter (Write it on his sheet.) and Jacob was a tent dweller, so he tended sheep and farmed. (Write this on his sheet.) Esau had to be brave to be a farmer. (Write "brave" on his sheet.) Jacob must have been very smart to have been a farmer. (Write "smart" on his sheet.) Esau was a good cook. (Write it on his sheet.) Jacob could build strong sturdy tents. (Add it to the list.) Esau was the oldest. (Write it on the list.) Jacob was the youngest. (Write it on the list.)

These twins weren't very much alike, were they? (Let the children respond.) That was the problem. They weren't alike and because they weren't alike, each thought he was the better person. Esau thought he was better because he had red hair and was a hunter and could cook and was brave and was the oldest. But Jacob thought he was better because he could farm and tend sheep and build tents and was smart and was the youngest. Now, I want you to decide which one really was the better of the two. (The children will most likely have a hard time deciding. Give two or three children time to tell which brother they think is better and why.)

It is hard to decide, isn't it? You know, just because we are different doesn't mean that one of us is better than another. God made Jacob and Esau very different but God didn't make one better than the other. If they had known that, I bet they would not have fought so much. But in almost every story about them in the Bible they are fighting and trying to prove that one is better than the other.

You have brothers and sisters. Are they just like you or different? (Let the children respond.) No two people are just alike. When you feel jealous of your brother or sister, remember Jacob and Esau and how special they each were because they were different. And remember all the fun they missed because they were always fighting and trying to outdo each other.

Closing Prayer

Dear God, we are each very special. We have special talents and abilities and we look different from each other.

Help us to remember that you made us different on purpose and that even though we are different, we are each very special. We pray in Christ's name. Amen.

Suggestions for Delivery

The key to making this sermon work is to keep the pace moving. Listing the qualities of each brother rather than having them written will peak the curiosity of the children as they wait to see what comes next. However, if this is done too slowly, they will get bored and you will lose their attention. I suggest that you have an index card with the characteristics listed as they will be on the poster boards rather than try to read it out of this book. This sermon also has several places for the children to respond. Remember that, depending on the particular ages and personalities of the children hearing it, the response time will vary. Always be prepared with answers and do not hesitate too long while waiting for responses. If your group is particularly outgoing and responsive, limit the responses so that the sermon does not drag out too long. Remember, attention spans can be very short and moving the story along will help.

Jacob Steals a Blessing

Scriptural Base: *Genesis 27:1-14*

Scriptural Summary

As Isaac, the father of Jacob and Esau, is sick and about to die, he calls Esau and asks him to go and catch a deer and make him stew from it. Then he will give Esau, the eldest son, his blessing—the blessing which God had given to Isaac. Rebekah overhears this and calls Jacob because she has decided Jacob should receive Isaac's blessing. She makes a stew and has Jacob wear fur on his arms and take the stew to Isaac. Isaac is nearly blind and when he feels the fur on Jacob's arms, he is tricked into believing that Jacob is Esau because Esau has hairy arms. Isaac then gives his blessing to Jacob, and once it is given it cannot be taken back. Jacob is promised all of the good things that life can offer. Jacob is pleased but poor Esau has lost his blessing because of the trick.

Learning Objectives

This sermon attempts to help the children understand how Jacob stole the blessing from Isaac and how important the blessing was to him. It also has the minor lesson that "tricks" can often hurt other people.

Materials Needed

A sheet of paper with "All the Good Things God Has to Offer" written on it. This should be rolled up and tied with string. You will also need a piece of furry material which can be wrapped around a child's arm. Esau was said to

17

have red hair so red is best but any color is fine. You will also need a blindfold.

The Sermon

Does anyone know anything about Jacob and Esau? (Give them time to recall anything they know.) Well, they were twin brothers who always fought! Their father was Isaac who had been blessed by God. Would one of you volunteer to be Isaac? (Choose a child and have him or her stand in the front.) Isaac, as I said, was blessed by God. And here is the blessing. (Give the child the blessing from God. This is the paper rolled up and tied.) When Isaac got very old, he knew he should pass the blessing on to his oldest son before he died. His oldest son was Esau. Now could one of you pretend to be Esau? (Choose a child.) Esau had very hairy arms so I am going to put this hair on you. (Put the furry material on Esau.) One day, Isaac called Esau to him and told him to go make him some special soup. He said that when Esau returned with the soup, he would bless him. But Rebekah, their mother, wanted Jacob to get the blessing, so she and Jacob worked out a plan. Would one of you be Jacob? (Choose a child to be Jacob.) And this is how the plan worked.

Isaac was sick and blind, so I am going to put this blindfold on him. (Put the blindfold on the child pretending to be Isaac.) Now, Isaac, Esau is going to come in and get his blessing. But to make sure it is him, you must feel of his hairy arms. So you will know it is Esau by his arms. (Then turn to the children and put your fingers on your lips as if to motion, "Shhh! Don't tell." Then take the fur off of Esau and put it on Jacob.) OK, Isaac, here comes your son Esau for his blessing. Now make sure it is him by feeling his hairy arms. (Let Isaac feel the fur.) Are you sure it is Esau? (Let Isaac respond.) OK, give him the blessing.

18

(Isaac gives the blessing to Jacob. The kids will probably be laughing by now. Take off the blindfold and put the fur back on Esau.)

Wait, Isaac, I thought you were supposed to give your blessing to Esau. Why does Jacob have it? (Isaac will be puzzled.) Isaac, you were tricked. Jacob put fur on his arms so you would think he was Esau. He tricked you and stole the blessing from Esau. That wasn't very nice, was it? Jacob, show us your blessing. (Have the child open the blessing and read it out loud.) Wow, that is a great blessing. But Esau is the oldest son and that was supposed to be his. What did you get Esau? Poor Esau got nothing. How do you think Esau felt? (They will say hurt and angry, etc.) You are right Esau was very, very angry and so Isaac left home and went to stay with his Uncle until Esau cooled down.

It was a very mean trick that Jacob played. Sometimes tricks are funny, but sometimes they hurt other people. This trick hurt Esau very much.

Closing Prayer:

Dear God, Jacob hurt Esau very much. I know that sometimes we hurt people. Sometimes we mean to hurt people. And sometimes we hurt people that we do not mean to hurt. Lord, help us to be kind to others and to think before we say or do things to hurt them. And when we do hurt them, remind us that we can ask them and you to forgive us. Amen.

Suggestions for Delivery

In order for the children to fully understand the trick Jacob plays on Esau, the children need to know which character is which. To make it a bit clearer you might want to make name tags for Isaac, Jacob, and Esau to wear. The children will probably think that the trick is funny especially when you are saying "Shhhh, and don't tell." Laughter is fine and you should be prepared for it. When you get to the part of the sermon when you say that some tricks are funny and some are not, they will quiet back down and be serious. So relax at the laughter.

Jacob Is Tricked into Marrying Leah

Scriptural Base: *Genesis 29:15-29*

Scriptural Summary

After Jacob tricks Esau out of his birthright and blessing, he flees to his Uncle Laban's where he plans to stay
until Esau's anger subsides. But when he sees Rachel,
Laban's youngest daughter, he falls in love. Laban
strikes a deal with Jacob and tells him that if he will
work for him for seven years, he can have Rachel as his
wife. Jacob agrees to this and when his seven years of
work are done, he has his wedding. But Laban secretly
sends Rachel's older sister Leah as the bride. Of course,
Jacob is very upset. So Laban tells him that he will give
him Rachel if he works for another seven years. Jacob
agrees and so he has two wives, the two daughters of
Laban.

Learning Objectives

This sermon helps the children act out the seven years
of work that Jacob had to do to earn his wife and then
shows the anger he felt when he was tricked. By using this
extremely active approach, the story should be remembered vividly by the children. It will also emphasize how
much love Jacob had for Rachel that he would work so
long to be able to marry her.

Materials Needed

A box with "Jacob's Bride" written on it and two pictures
of brides cut from a magazine. One should have "Rachel"

written on it and the other have "Leah" written on it. They should both be inside the box.

The Sermon

Today I want to tell you a story about a man named Jacob who went to stay at his uncle's distant home. The uncle was named Laban and he had two daughters, Leah and Rachel, her younger sister. Jacob fell in love with Rachel and told Laban he would work seven years for him if at the end of that time he could have Rachel as his wife. Laban agreed. Rachel was very beautiful and while Jacob worked hard he kept thinking about how happy he would be to marry Rachel. He could imagine what she looked like. (Hold up a picture of her.) But he couldn't have her until he worked his seven years. (Put the picture in the box labeled "Jacob's Bride.")

Now I want you to pretend that you are Jacob. I am going to tell you what work you have to do and then you act it out. The first thing you have to do is chop wood. Let's pretend we are chopping wood. (Let them do that for a few seconds.) Next you have to gather the sheep. (Have the children run in place.) Next you have to repair the roof. (Have the children pretend to hammer in nails.) Next you have to work in the garden. (Have the children to hoe in the garden.) And last, you have to bale the hay. (Have the children to bale hay with a pitchfork.) Are you tired? (Give them time to respond.) Well guess what? That was only the first year. You promised to work for Laban for seven years. But you really want to marry Rachel so it is worth it.

(Repeat the words and actions six more times, pausing between each year to remind the children that this is very hard work but worth it for Rachel. By the time they do it six more times, they will be tired.)

All right, that was hard work! And now here is your bride. (Pull out the picture of the bride with Leah written on it. The kids will be surprised.) Wait a minute. Something is wrong! Laban tricked you. You worked all those seven years and instead of getting Rachel, your true love, you got Leah. What are you going to do? (Let them respond.) Those are all good ideas, but the Bible tells us that Jacob simply made another deal with Laban. In Bible times men were allowed to have two wives. And so Jacob agreed to work seven more years in exchange for Rachel. Are you ready to work? (They will moan and say no.) No, you don't have to act out seven more years of work. But poor Jacob did. He worked fourteen years for Rachel. That is a lot of work. He must have loved Rachel very much.

Closing Prayer

Dear God, Jacob must have loved Rachel very much to have worked so hard for her. When we hear this story we think about people we love, our moms and dads and friends and brothers and sisters. Bless each of them and help us to do for them whatever they need out of love for them. Amen.

Suggestions for Delivery

This sermon is action packed and must be done with energy and enthusiasm so that the children will have that same energy as they work. I suggest writing the five actions done each year on an index card so that your hands will be free from the book. Then as each year passes, work faster and faster so that the children have to work harder. Remember the more fun you have, the more involved the children will become. If possible, you should do the actions with the children to make it easier to keep the story moving.

Wrestling with God

Scriptural Base: *Genesis 32:22-32*

Scriptural Summary

As Jacob is returning home he hears that his brother Esau is coming with hundreds of men to meet him. Because Jacob had stolen Esau's blessing many years before, Jacob thinks Esau is coming to kill him. But during the night God and Jacob wrestle and Jacob is injured and limps away. As a result of coming face to face with God, Jacob knows that he is blessed by God. From that time on he is a faithful follower and no longer the trickster he had once been. He is now ready to face his brother, his past wrongs, and go on with his adult life.

Learning Objectives

There are many times in children's lives when they fail to live up to expectations of those around them, when they lie, or break something that is not theirs, or even cheat. These can be difficult times for children. This sermon, through the use of a repeated chorus, helps prepare children for those times when they must face those people whom they have wronged. By telling them the story of Jacob and his wrestling with God about his past, the children will hopefully feel a sense of not being alone. They will also discover that praying about it, talking it over—even wrestling with God—will help them do what they must.

Materials Needed

None

The Sermon

Today I want to tell you a story about Jacob and a very long
night he spent alone. Jacob had been in hiding a very long
time from his brother who he had done some mean things
to. He finally felt like he should grow up and go home, but
he was afraid of his brother. He was afraid that Esau would
still be angry with him and maybe even kill him. So God
came to Jacob and wrestled with him all night long and gave
him courage to face his brother and all his mistakes.

Now I would like to tell you that story in a sort of poem.
I will say a part, and I will end it by saying, "When you have
a hard decision," and you will finish that line by saying,
"Pray, talk, or wrestle with God about it." Let's practice
once. (Have the children complete the sentence.) Good,
now here we go.

Once there was a man named Jacob who had done many
mean things to his brother Esau, and he knew the time
had come to face his brother and apologize. But he wasn't
sure that this was the right time to do it. You see, he had a
hard decision and when you have a hard decision (*children
respond*).

So he sent his wives and children away and he spent the
night alone because he had a hard decision and when you
have a hard decision (*children respond*).

Jacob went to sleep, but while he slept God appeared and
wrestled with him all night, trying to help Jacob figure out
the right thing to do. Because he had a hard decision and
when you have a hard decision (*children respond*).

And so they wrestled and wrestled until it was almost day. It
was a hard fight—so hard that Jacob got his leg hurt. But
he had to keep wrestling because when you have a hard
decision (*children respond*).

25

Finally day had come, and Jacob knew the time to face his brother was there, but before God left, God blessed Jacob in a special way because God knew Jacob would do the right thing. When you have a hard decision (*children respond*).

After the night with God, Jacob was ready to face Esau and everything turned out fine. He was glad he had wrestled with God about it because when you have a hard decision (*children respond*).

You know, Jacob isn't the only one who has hard decisions. Did you know that children and adults have hard decisions as well and when they have a hard decision (*children respond*).

Once a little girl named Amy broke a special lamp of her mommy's that she was never supposed to touch. She didn't know if she should tell her mommy the truth about breaking it. It was a hard decision and when you have a hard decision (*children respond*).

Once there was a little boy named Timmy who cheated on a spelling test and felt very badly about it. He wanted to ask his teacher if he could take it over again, but he was afraid that she might be angry with him. Timmy had a hard decision and when you have a hard decision (*children respond*).

One day Alex and Sammy were playing dress up in their sister's room and Alex found a watch he really liked. Sammy found a ring she really liked and so they decided to keep them. But later their sister was very upset to find the watch and ring missing. Alex and Sammy felt bad but they liked the watch and ring so much they didn't want to give them back. They had a hard decision and when you have a hard decision (*children respond*).

Jacob had a very hard decision, and we have hard decisions too! And always remember, when you have a hard decision (*children respond*).

Closing Prayer

God, who is always there when we need to talk, please help us through our difficult times. We try to do what is best, but sometimes we goof up and make mistakes. In those times, help us to remember that you are there with us and will help us figure out the best and the correct thing to do. We pray in the name of Jesus. Amen.

Suggestions for Delivery

This sermon will work nicely if you keep the poem moving and do not stop or elaborate between responses. I deliberately did not say what the correct thing to do in each of the situations would be so that the children would wrestle with that themselves.

I chose names at random for the children's names in the poem. The use of a name makes the situations seem more real to the children. However, I would suggest that you try not to use a name of a child in your group. Feel free to change the name if you have an Amy, Timmy, Alex, or Sammy in your group. Children tease each other and it would be a shame if a child got teased because that child's name was used in the sermon.

Jacob's New Name

Scriptural Base: *Genesis 35:1-12*

Scriptural Summary

After Jacob's rather doubtful childhood, he has proved by this time in the Scripture that he is indeed a follower of the will of God. He is no longer the trickster he was. He has faced his past and mended his relationship with Esau. He is now the man of God we think of most often when we think of Jacob, the descendant of Abraham and Isaac. God also has seen the change in Jacob and decides to change his name from Jacob to Israel. God gives Jacob the same blessing and promise that was given to Abraham and Isaac.

Learning Objectives

Growing up is wondrous and exciting time for children. It can also be a time of change and children, like most people, are sometimes afraid of change. This sermon stresses that God is in the midst of change and blesses it and finds it exciting and above all—good. Using movement and mime, this sermon enacts many of the changes that we go through and that we see in the world around us.

This sermon will speak to the preteens and teens in the congregation who are beginning puberty and all the physical and emotional changes associated with being teens and growing up.

Materials Needed

None

28

The Sermon

Have you ever noticed that some things in nature change a lot as they grow up? And they have one name when they are young and another when they get big. Today I want us to pretend that we are some things in nature. I'll say a name and you become it. Then when I say it grows up you can change into that. Watch me and I'll help you. The first thing I want us to pretend to be is a caterpillar. Can you crawl like a caterpillar? (Give the children time to crawl.) And when caterpillars grow up they change into butterflies. Can you pretend to turn into butterflies? (Give them time.) Great! Now let's pretend to be tadpoles. Can you pretend to swim like a tiny tadpole? (Give them time to pretend.) What do tadpoles turn into? (Let the children respond.) Yes, frogs. Can you pretend to be a frog? (Give them time.)

Now let's pretend to be acorns. An acorn is sort of a seed. What do you think it would look like if you were an acorn? (Give them time.) Good. Now an acorn turns into a big oak tree. (Let them pretend to be trees.)

You know acorns and tadpoles and caterpillars aren't the only things that change. We change too. First we are babies. Can you be a baby? (Give them time to pretend they are babies.) Then we grow bigger and bigger until we are adults and grown up. Let me see you grow up from a baby to an adult. (Give them time.)

Thank you, you can sit down. In the Bible there is a story of a little boy who grew up from a baby to a teen and finally to a man. His name was Jacob and when he was all grown up, God was happy with what kind of person Jacob had become. So God changed his name from Jacob to Israel and gave him a wonderful blessing because he was so proud. Someday each of you will grow up, and you will go through many changes. Some of these changes you will like and others you will not. But just like Jacob, God will be with you as you grow up and when you are grown God will be very proud of you. We don't get a new name like tadpoles and acorns get, or even like Jacob got, but we will grow and change and God will watch us and care for us every step of the way.

Closing Prayer

God, growing up is fun most of the time, but sometimes it is scary. Please be with us, reminding us with new change that you are proud of us and love us and that we are becoming the people you want us to be. We pray in the name of your son. Amen.

Suggestions for Delivery

The children will most likely enjoy this sermon. However, if your group tends to be shy, you might have to do the motions with them to help them feel confident. It will help to choose leaders ahead of time and go over the pretend things with them so that at least part of your group will do it.

I suggest that you keep the pace going. The children will be cute acting out butterflies, and the other things, but you do not want their attention spans to wear out before the end of the sermon. So keep the pace up and enjoy them. We all like to act and to get attention. Don't be afraid to let them know that you think they are great for being free enough to pretend and have fun.

Ruth, a Faithful Follower of God

Ruth Is Faithful to Naomi

Scriptural Base: *Ruth 1*

Scriptural Summary:

Naomi and Elimelech have two sons and when Elimelech dies, Naomi is taken care of by her sons. The sons both marry. One wife is named Orpah and the other Ruth. Then the two sons die. So poor Naomi has lost both her husband and her two sons. She is not sure how any of them, now widowed, can survive, so she begs her two daughters-in-law to return home to their mothers' homes. Both resist, but Orpah finally goes home. Ruth, however, refuses to leave Naomi alone and gives Naomi a pledge of her devotion and love. The two women return to Naomi's hometown, Bethlehem.

Learning Objectives

The story of Ruth and Naomi is one of powerful love and faithfulness. It is this love that children are brought into as they become part of a church family. In this sermon, using motions as well as the words of Ruth, the children will begin to understand what it means to say that we are all part of God's family. It stresses the idea that we are bound together in love and that we can depend on each other at all times.

The closing prayer emphasizes the need to be a faithful, loving person when others need you as well as always depending on others when you need them.

31

This sermon could be used on a Sunday when someone is baptized and is publicly joining the family of God.

Materials Needed:

None

The Sermon

Do any of you know a loving story in the Bible? (Give the children time to share and then be prepared to mention some examples: when Jesus healed people, or when Jesus raised Lazarus from the dead, or some of the parables about love.) Well, today I want to tell you a story about the love of one woman for her mother-in-law. And I think it is one of the most loving stories in the whole Bible.

Once there was a woman and her husband and they had two sons who both got married. The woman's name was Naomi and, sadly enough, her husband and both her sons died. In Bible times when a woman's husband and sons died she had no job or money or way to take care of herself. So Naomi and her sons' wives were left with nowhere to go and very little money. Naomi told her daughters-in-law to go back home to their parents where they could be taken care of. They both felt badly about leaving Naomi, but Naomi insisted. So one of them, Orpah, left and went home. But Ruth, the other daughter-in-law, would not leave Naomi. She told Naomi that she loved her and that she was part of her family now and would always be with her and care about her.

It would have been a lot easier for Ruth to leave Naomi, but she chose to stay because she loved Naomi. The words Ruth spoke to Naomi were almost like a poem. I want you to say them after me. I will say a line and do a motion and then you repeat it.

These are the words Ruth used to tell Naomi how much she loved her. Here we go.

Where you go (put hands out, palms up) I will go (put hands on heart)
(*children repeat*)
And where you stay (point to floor about two feet in front of you) I will stay. (point at your feet)
(*children repeat*)
Your people (move hands palms up as if indicating a huge crowd) are my people. (reverse the motion so that you are pointing to yourself again)
(*children repeat*)
Your God (point index finger up towards the sky) is my God. (raise both arms up as if pronouncing a benediction)
(*children repeat*)
Where you die, (place one cheek on hands as if sleeping on a pillow) I will die. (place hands on the other cheek)
(*children repeat*)
And there I will be buried. (place arms and hands at sides)
(*children repeat*)
I swear a solemn oath before God, (lift right hand as if being sworn in at a trial)
(*children repeat*)
Nothing but death shall divide us. (clinch hands together tightly in front of you)
(*children repeat*)

I was thinking about these words and about being a Christian. You know we as Christians are part of a special family—our church family. And so we are all brothers and sisters. I think the words that Ruth said should be words we speak to each other. Wouldn't it be wonderful if we loved each other as much as Ruth loved Naomi?

Let's get into a circle and say the words to each other. (Form the children into a circle and repeat the above passage.)

Closing Prayer

God of love, we thank you for this story about Ruth and Naomi. We also thank you that we are a part of this church family and that we have people who love us and will support us no matter what comes along. This is a wonderful gift. And, God, help us to remember that as part of your family, we must be loving toward each other. When it is hard to feel loving and caring, please help us remember Ruth and the wonderful love she had for Naomi. We pray in the name of your loving son, our Lord. Amen.

Suggestions for Delivery

This sermon begins by telling the story of Ruth and Naomi. It should be told with enthusiasm and excitement to keep the children's attention. It will also help to keep their attention if you look up from the book. The more familiar with the story you are, the more eye contact you can have—and children respond so well to eye contact! When having the children repeat the poem and motions it is best to not let much time pass between when they end their part and you start a new line. Also, it will probably be best to repeat the line and motion with them just to keep it going and to help them stay together. If you are using this for a baptism Sunday children's sermon, it would work well to have the person or persons baptized join the circle. As they do tell the children that when a person is baptized, they are publicly becoming a part of the church family.

Ruth Finds a Friend—Boaz

Scriptural Base: *Ruth 2*

Scriptural Summary

Ruth and her mother-in-law, Naomi, are having a hard time since the death of their husbands. They have no jobs or food. So Ruth decides to go to a field and glean after the reapers. She ends up in the field of her kinsman, Boaz. While she is gathering grain, Boaz comes to the fields and sees her. He has heard of her kindness and dedication to Naomi and tells her to take all she wants. He instructs the reapers to be kind to her. When she returns home and tells Naomi all about his kindness, Naomi says a blessing for him. Ruth gleans many days from his field.

Learning Objectives

In this active sermon the children will learn the story of Boaz and the kindness he showed to Ruth. They will also learn the concept of sharing what we have in excess with others who are less fortunate. They will learn this by actually gleaning from a field which will be created.

Materials Needed

A can of popcorn and several clear baggies. Sandwich bags will be fine.

The Sermon

In the Bible is a story of two women, Ruth and Naomi. Their husbands had died and in Bible times that was very bad because women didn't have jobs and had a very hard time supporting themselves. Well, these two women were in a mess and did not have enough food. So Ruth had an idea. She decided to go to a field and glean after the farmers. Do any of you know what it is to glean? (Give them time to answer but most won't know what it is.)

Gleaning was a way that the farmers would share their extra food with the poor people who didn't have any food. Let me show you what gleaning was. First, I need someone to volunteer to pretend to be the farmer, Boaz. (Choose a child.) Now, Boaz, you own this farm and here is your seed. (Give the child the can of popcorn.) Very carefully I want you to place this popcorn in four piles on the floor. (Give the child time to do it. Make sure it is fairly well spread out.) Very good. OK, the field is planted. Let's pretend that it grows up and it is now time to harvest—time to pick the crop. In the story it is wheat, so let's pretend that our field is covered with wheat ready to be picked.

Boaz, I want you to choose three people to work for you and to harvest this crop. (Let Boaz choose three people.) The three of you work for Boaz and you are going to harvest the wheat for him. Now I will give you each a bag and you have to pick up one kernel of popcorn at a time and put it in your bag. You have to bend over, pick it up, stand up and place it in your bag. Then you do it again and again until the time is up. And remember, try and pick up as much popcorn as you can. Also, you can only work at one pile at a time. So all of you start at this first pile and pick it up. When I say move on, you must move to a different pile until you have picked at all four piles. (Make sure they understand how it works.)

Oh, I almost forgot, there is one other person in the field. Her name is Ruth. Would one of you like to pretend to be Ruth? (Choose a child to be Ruth and give her a bag.) Ruth, you have no food and are very poor. So after

36

the workers leave a pile of food, you may pick up whatever you want to. But you can only pick up food from the piles that they have finished. Do you understand?

Boaz, you own the field, so tell your workers to begin, and I'll shout and tell them when it is time to move on to a new pile. (Boaz tells them to begin. You watch and when about three-fourths of the popcorn is picked up, shout for them to move on and let Ruth begin gleaning. Continue until all four piles have been harvested.)

Well, workers, it is time to show Boaz what you did. Boaz, what do you think of the first worker's harvest? (Give him time to say good.) How about your second worker's harvest? (Give him time to react.) And how about your third worker's harvest? (Give him time to react.) I agree, all of the workers did a great job. Hey, wait a minute Boaz. Did you hire Ruth? Why did she get some of the harvest? (Boaz will not be sure.) In the Bible, people like Ruth who were poor gleaned after the workers. They followed behind like Ruth did and picked up the left over and missed wheat. So what do you think Boaz thought about this? Do you think he liked it or thought it was unfair? After all it was his field, he owned the grain. (Let the children respond. They will probably have mixed reactions.)

In the story, Boaz had heard of the love and care Ruth had had for her mother-in-law Naomi, and he felt sorry for them. So he told his workers to be kind to Ruth. Boaz, tell your workers to be kind. (Boaz tells them.) And he told Ruth to glean grain from his fields any time she wanted to. Boaz tell Ruth. (He tells her.) In fact, Boaz liked Ruth so much that he went back to his workers and told them to even drop some extra wheat for Ruth to find. Boaz was certainly a good friend to Ruth. And when Ruth went home and told Naomi about this kind friend, Naomi asked God to always bless Boaz.

37

Closing Prayer

Dear God, thank you for this story of Boaz and Ruth and gleaning. We have many extra things in our lives, extra food, clothes we have outgrown, extra money. Help us to realize that there are poor people like Ruth and Naomi in our world today. Help us to be generous and share what we have. For like Boaz, when we give to others who have less than we do, your special blessing is on us. Thank you for all we have and for our willingness to share. In the name of Jesus. Amen.

Suggestions for Delivery

This sermon might seem complicated at first, but it is actually very simple to do and very effective. The children have the opportunity to actually learn about gleaning by doing it and seeing it done. The most important factor in delivering this sermon is making sure the children know what they are doing. It is probably wise to walk through the harvesting process once before they actually harvest just to make sure they know what to do.

The child you choose for Boaz needs to be a fairly outgoing child so that he will speak up and say what you tell him to say.

Also, you need to carefully notice how much popcorn is being harvested so that there will be some left over for Ruth to glean. The sermon will not work unless Ruth has a harvest as well as the workers.

Ruth Marries Boaz

Scriptural Base: *Ruth 3:1–4:12*

Scriptural Summary

Ruth and Naomi are both widowed and have no place to turn. So Naomi suggests to Ruth that she go to her kinsman, Boaz, and ask him to take her in as his wife. She does this by lying at his feet, and he is glad to take her. However, he is an honest man and knows that there is another man in town who is a closer relative. It was the custom that the closest kin would have the first choice. So Boaz goes to the kin and asks him if he wants Ruth. That kinsman is already married and says no. So the kinsman takes off his sandal as a symbol to Boaz that he can marry Ruth. Boaz then gladly marries Ruth. Ruth and Naomi have a home and security, and Boaz has done what is right in the eyes of God.

Learning Objectives

The customs of the people in Bible times often seem foreign and silly to children. This sermon attempts to teach the children that many of the customs seem odd but are much like customs we have today. It also helps the children learn an often confusing story but one that is about great love and about doing what is proper.

Materials Needed

A pair of sandals that a child could slip on over his or her shoes; a piece of paper that says "job application" on top of it; and another piece that says, "Contract" across the top of it. Also you will need a pencil.

The Sermon

Today I want to tell you a story about Ruth and Boaz. Now these two people lived a very, very long time ago. They lived in Bible times even before Jesus was born. And you know that was a long time ago. Some of the things they did seem sort of strange to us today. But actually, many of the things they did are like things we do today. Let me show you as I tell you the story of Ruth and Boaz.

Our story begins with Ruth whose husband has died. She lives with her mother-in-law who also has no husband. Today when a woman's husband dies, she might go and get a job to support herself. I need two girl volunteers to be "Ruth of Today" and "Ruth of Bible times." (Choose two girls and have them stand where all the children can see.) So Ruth finds herself without a husband. The "Ruth of today" might go out and find a job. Here is a job application. Pretend to be filling it out. (Hand the job application and pencil to one of the girls.) But the "Ruth of Bible times" couldn't get a job because women weren't allowed to work, so poor Ruth had nothing to do but beg for food and help. (Have the other Ruth beg for food.)

Very good. Now in our story, Naomi, Ruth's mother-in-law, has an idea. She tells Ruth to go to a relative and ask him to marry her. How do we ask people to marry us today? (Let the children respond.) I need two boys to be Boaz, the relative of Ruth. (Choose two boys.) OK, one of you is the "Boaz of Today" and the other one is the "Boaz of Bible times." Now "Ruth of Today," I want you to pose like you are proposing to Boaz. Get down on one knee and pretend to be asking him. That is how we would propose today. But in Bible times, Ruth proposed to Boaz by lying down at his feet. (Have the other Ruth lie at Boaz's feet.)

So, Ruth proposes to Boaz. He wants to marry her, but he remembers that another relative should get to decide first if he wants her. So Boaz goes to the relative. I need two volunteers. One to be the "Relative of Today" and one to be the "Relative of Bible Times." (Choose the children and have the Bible-time relative put on the sandals.) Boaz goes to his relative and asks if he wants to marry Ruth. The relative says he can't and he wants to make it known that he gives Boaz permission to marry Ruth. Now today, Boaz and this next of kin might sign a contract saying that the relative gives Boaz permission to marry Ruth. So you can give Boaz the contract to sign. (Let them pretend to sign the contract.) But in Bible times, the relative gave permission to Boaz by giving him his sandal. (Have the child give his sandal to Boaz.) And so Boaz married Ruth and God blessed him. If Boaz had not married her, Ruth and Naomi would not have had any money or food or a place to stay. He did the right thing.

Some of those Bible-time customs seem weird, don't they? Which ones seemed weird to you? (Let the children respond.) People in Bible times did some things differently than we do today, but one thing is the same. Boaz tried to do what God wanted him to do. And we try to do that today, too. Perhaps some of the customs we follow today will seem strange to people who live many years in the future. But, as Christians, people will always try to do what God wants them to do.

Closing Prayer

Dear God, we try so hard to do what you want us to do. Please guide us and help us to do what you want. Also remind us when we mess up that you still love us and forgive us and will allow us to begin trying to do what you want all over again. For like Boaz, we want to live the way you want us to and follow close beside you always. In the name of Christ. Amen.

Suggestions for Delivery

This sermon attempts to show differences in customs while at the same time telling the story of Ruth and Boaz. It is important to keep the pace up so that the children don't forget the story as you choose kids to be parts and set them up. As you tell the story, place the children where you want them and try to keep the story going instead of stopping to explain where they should stand, and so forth.

Naomi, an Understanding Mother-in-law

Scriptural Base: *Ruth 4:13-22*

Scriptural Summary

Boaz and Ruth are married and now he assumes responsibility for both Ruth and Naomi, her mother-in-law. Soon after they marry, Ruth conceives a child, and when he is born they name him Obed. Naomi takes his child, who is not really her own blood and becomes his nurse and finds great joy in him. This continues the lineage which will eventually lead to David.

Learning Objectives

Naomi could have been jealous of Ruth's child since he is the child of another man (besides her son) and because he is not her actual blood relative. But instead, she chose to love and care for Obed. This is similar to the reaction we are supposed to have at a baptismal ceremony as a person publicly becomes part of our church family. This sermon attempts to stress to the children that, as Christians, we must love others as if they are our own flesh and blood. This sermon also, in an indirect way, deals with the feelings that some children may experience as part of a blended family, where they might feel jealous of a half brother or sister or a step sibling.

Materials Needed

A baby doll wrapped in a blanket.

43

The Sermon

Today, I want to tell you a story from the Bible about a woman who had a big decision to make, and I want you to really think about the decision she might make. There was a woman named Naomi. Could one of you pretend to be Naomi? (Choose a child to be Naomi.) Now Naomi's son married a woman named Ruth. Would one of you pretend to be Ruth? (Choose a child to be Ruth.) And I am sure that like most mothers-in-law, Naomi dreamed of the day that Ruth would hand her a baby and say, "Here is your grandchild, Naomi!" Let's do that. Ruth, here is a baby. (Give the doll to Ruth.) Now give it to Naomi and say, "Here is your grandchild." (Let them do it.) How do you think Naomi would have felt? (Give the children time to respond.) I am sure Naomi would have been very, very happy to have a grandchild. But in this story, something terrible happens. Ruth's husband, Naomi's son, died. Ruth stays with Naomi and treats her well and then Ruth marries another man, Boaz. Ruth and Boaz have a baby. One day Ruth hands her baby to Naomi and says, "Look at my baby." But Naomi knows it isn't really her grandchild, because Boaz is not her son. Let's do that. Ruth hand the baby to Naomi again. (Let Ruth give the doll to Naomi.) How do you think Naomi felt this time? (Let the children respond.) Naomi could have been sad because this wasn't her own grandchild. Or she could have felt angry at Ruth for loving another man. Or she could have felt disappointed. But do you know how Naomi felt? She felt very, very happy, and she cared for and loved the baby like it was her own grandchild.

You know, some of us may have step brothers and sisters who aren't really our brothers and sisters but we are expected to love them. Sometimes it is hard and we don't want to. That would be a good time to remember this story.

And did you know that Christians are supposed to be the family of God? When someone comes to our church as a visitor and then decides to join our church, we are supposed to treat them as one of the family. But sometimes we don't know them and don't want to. That would be a good time to remember this story.

And did you know that every time a person is baptized, the minister turns to the congregation and asks us if we will love and care for them as if they were part of our own family? That would be a good time to remember this story.

Naomi had a big decision to make. She could be jealous of Ruth's baby because it wasn't her son's child or she could love it as if it were her own. She chose to love and care for him. You will have moments of decision like Naomi, and at times like that, I hope you will remember this story and the love Naomi had.

Closing Prayer

Dear God, it is not always easy to love others as ourselves. Help us to be more loving and accepting of others. Help us to love others as you have loved us first. We pray remembering all the love Jesus showed to strangers and to us. Amen.

Suggestions for Delivery

This sermon is very simple so the delivery should be fairly simple. However, notice that when you give examples of times when the children might be asked to love people they don't even like or are jealous of, I suggest that you not tell them what to do, but rather remind them that this is a story they might remember at such a time. The decision to love or not will come from their own hearts. Be careful, then, not to become too judgmental or preachy in the closing part of the sermon.

Samuel, a Prophet of God

Hannah Asks God for a Baby

Scriptural Base: *I Samuel 1:1-20*

Scriptural Summary

Hannah and Elkanah are married. His other wife has had children but poor Hannah has not. She is terribly upset about having no children. When Elkanah and his two wives go to the temple to make a sacrifice, Hannah is deeply distressed and prays to God to please give her a baby. She promises God that if she has a baby, she will give him to the Lord and, as a sign of that promise, she will never cut his hair. While Hannah is praying, Eli, the priest, watches and thinks that she is drunk. He tells her to leave but she explains to him that she is not drunk and tells him of her desire to have a baby. Eli blesses her. And when Hannah returns home she becomes pregnant and conceives a son whom she names Samuel, which means, "I asked the Lord."

Learning Objectives

Through the use of a game very similar to charades, the children will discover the many emotions that Hannah felt when she was trying to have a baby and praying and hoping for it. She had all the emotions that people have when they want something very much and ask God for it. Sometimes children feel ashamed for feeling angry or frustrated when praying to God. But when we pray to God, we bring

46

our whole selves before God. This sermon shows that when we pray, we (like Hannah) can feel whatever we feel and don't need to be ashamed to show God. God wants us to come and tell all about our problems, joys, or whatever we feel. This sermon stresses the importance of being ourselves with God.

Materials Needed

A box or basket with slips of paper with one of the following emotions written on each one: happy, sad, frustrated, desperate, angry, extremely happy, tired, disappointed.

The Sermon

Did you ever want anything very, very badly? What? (Give the children time to respond.) How did you feel when you wanted something and never got it? (Give them time to respond.) And how did you feel when you got it? (Give them time to respond.) Did you ever want something so badly that you prayed for it? (Give them time to share.)

Our scripture lesson is about a woman named Hannah who was married to a man named Elkanah. Hannah was very sad because she did not have any children. She and her husband had tried to have a baby but just couldn't. Every year they went to the Temple in Jerusalem to pray, and every year Hannah asked God for the same thing. Do you know what she prayed for? (Let them guess, a baby.) You are right, she asked for a baby.

But it took God a very long time to answer her prayer. And while she prayed, she felt many different emotions, just like you feel different emotions when you want something very badly. So today, I want us to see some of the emotions that Hannah felt. I have a basket here with slips of paper inside. Each slip of paper has an emotion written on it. I will choose one of you to draw an emotion out of this basket and act it out. Then the rest of you will try to guess what the emotion is.

(One by one, have the children draw an emotion and act it out. As the children guess correctly, say, "Yes, _____ is an emotion that Hannah felt while she prayed to God.")

You all did such a good job acting out emotions and guessing what they were. Hannah sure felt a lot of emotions. Some were happy emotions and some were sad, angry emotions. Did you know that Hannah got so emotional that Eli, a priest who lived in the temple, thought she was drunk? That is pretty emotional, huh?

Well, each time she prayed, Hannah asked God for a baby and promised that if God would give her one, she would give her baby to the Lord's service. And do you know what happened? She had a baby son and named him Samuel, which means, "I asked the Lord."

We will all be like Hannah someday. Someday, we will want something so badly that we will pray for it. And we will have many of the same feelings that Hannah had. And some of our prayers will be answered, and we will feel happy like Hannah. Some of our prayers will not be answered the way we want, and we will be sad and upset like Hannah was.

Do you think God got mad at Hannah because she was so emotional when she prayed? (Give them time to respond.) I don't think God was upset, I think God understood her feelings. Did you know there are some people who believe that you should only pray when you are happy? There are some people who think that God gets mad if we share how we really feel? What do you think Hannah would say to those people? (Let the children respond.) I like the story of Hannah because she shows us that it is all right to tell God exactly how we feel. And whether you feel happy, sad, angry, frustrated or just tired, you can always pray to God, just like Hannah did.

Closing Prayer

Dear God, we all feel something different right now. Some of us feel angry, some feel tired, some feel bored, and some feel happy. Thank you for giving us feelings and thank you for stories like the one about Hannah that shows us that feelings are OK to have and that you are always there to listen to us when we pray. We pray in the name of Jesus, your son. Amen.

Suggestions for Delivery

The children will probably like the game of charades and emotions. In order to keep their energy focused, keep the game moving along. Give them time to guess but not too much time so that they get bored. I also would not spend a great deal of time on the first part of the sermon. Just use that to warm them up. Then give them time at the end to talk about their reactions to the story and all the emotions of Hannah.

Samuel Lives with Eli

Scriptural Base: *I Samuel 1:21–2:10*

Scriptural Summary

While Hannah tried to conceive a son, she would pray to God and promise that if God would give her a child, she would see that his whole life was spent serving God. So after she has Samuel, she weans him and then takes him to the temple and gives him into the care of Eli, the priest, to be raised as a servant of God. She then sings a song of praise to God.

Learning Objectives

Hannah had made a promise or vow to God and she kept it. We can only assume that this was a difficult promise to keep. But she joyfully keeps her promise. This sermon stresses the importance of keeping our promises even when that is sometimes hard to do. It also stresses the faithfulness of a woman who could give her child to God. This is a true story of faith which children need to have stored in their minds for difficult times in adulthood, even if they do not understand it yet.

Materials Needed

Two eggs and a bowl to break them in and a small towel to clean up with. Also, glue and masking tape and string.

The Sermon

Did you ever hear the nursery tale of Humpty Dumpty? Humpty Dumpty was an egg (hold up one egg) who fell off a wall (drop egg into the pan) and could not be put back together again. Did you ever try to put an egg back together again? (Let the children respond.) I have some glue and tape and string. Do you think we could put this egg back together again? Let's try. (Give a few children a turn trying to put the egg back together again.)

It's no use. Once an egg is broken there is no putting it back together, is there? (Let the children respond.) Well did you know that there is a woman in the Bible named Hannah who once made a promise to God and once she had made it, she couldn't take it back? It was sort of like an egg. Hannah wanted a baby so badly that she prayed and prayed for it and begged God to give her a baby. And she said, "God, if you give me a baby, I will make sure that his whole life is lived in service to you." She made a promise to God. (Hold up the egg.) Once she had made the promise there was no turning back. Once you make a promise you can't take it back. (Drop the egg in the bowl.) And God heard Hannah's prayer and gave her a child. Hannah remembered her promise and she knew that she had to take her baby to another city and leave him to grow up in the temple with Eli, a priest, so that he could learn to serve God. That would be a hard promise to keep! I bet she wanted to take that promise back and say, "Never mind, God. Forget I said that!" But just like this broken egg, there was no way to take it back.

So she took her baby, Samuel, to Eli the priest and left him there. How do you think Hannah felt leaving her baby? (Give the children time to respond.) Well the Bible tells us that she knew how important promises were and so she was happy to do what she had promised. She must have felt a bit sad and upset, but she knew she was doing the right thing. So she sings a prayer to God and says, "My heart rejoices in the Lord."

You and I make promises sometimes. And sometimes when we make promises, a little time passes and we wish we had not promised. And when those times happen to you, I want you to remember Hannah and the promise that she kept. She felt so good about keeping her promise that she sang a happy song. It isn't always easy to keep our promises, but if you do I'll bet, like Hannah, you will be glad you did and even sing a happy song.

Closing Prayer

O God, promises are not easy to keep. Sometimes we promise and then don't feel like keeping it. Help us to remember this story at those times and remind us of how important keeping our promises are. Thank you for your promise to us that you will always love and care for us. We have a hard time keeping promises sometimes, but we know that you never have a problem keeping your promise of love to us. Thank you. We pray in the name of your loving son. Amen.

Suggestions for Delivery

The children will probably like the beginning of the story and will enjoy trying to put the egg back together. Let them have enough time to really try to put it back together, but remember that that is only a small part of the sermon. So keep the sermon moving by holding up another egg. This motion will probably quiet them as they will know what is coming. They will probably quiet down because they will want to see the second egg broken.

If you feel that the children hearing this story might interpret it to mean that someday their mom or dad might give them away, you might want to say something before you begin the story of Hannah like, "Now, before I begin this story, I want you to remember that what Hannah did, promising to give her son to God, is not anything your parents would ever do. And it is not anything that God would ask for!" Or you might want to insert a similar statement just before the closing prayer.

Hannah Makes a Coat for Samuel

Scriptural Base: *I Samuel 2:18-20*

Scriptural Summary:

Because of her promise to God, Hannah has had to leave Samuel with Eli the priest in the temple. She visits him once a year and when she does she takes him a coat which she makes for him.

Learning Objectives

This sermon helps the children understand that the gift of a coat made by Hannah was more than just a simple coat—it was an act of love and deep care. This sermon emphasizes to the children that even very simple acts, like decorating a paper heart, can show deep love for someone.

Materials Needed

A paper heart for each child and a crayon for each child.

The Sermon

Our scripture lesson today is about a woman, Hannah, and her son, Samuel, who lives away from her. Samuel lives in a temple with a man named Eli. Each year Hannah makes her son a coat and takes it to Samuel. Can you guess why? (Let the children guess. Throw out ideas like, "he might have been cold" or "children grow very quickly and he probably outgrew his last year's coat.") There are many reasons that Hannah took her son the coat. But I think the biggest reason is that she loved him. There are lots of ways to show people we love them. We can hug them, or tell them we love them or write them notes. Those are all good ways to show love. But today, I want to give each of you a chance to show someone you love how much you love them by making them a gift. I have a paper heart and crayons for each of you. I want you to decorate the heart any way you want. And when your gift is finished, you will be able to give it to someone you really love. (Pass out the hearts and give them time to decorate them.)

When you are finished, please put your crayon back in the box, and take your heart to someone in the room you love very much. (Let them give their gifts away.)

Would all of you who got a gift please stand? (Let them stand.) See the looks on their faces? They feel very loved, don't they? (Let the children respond.) Each year Hannah made her son a little coat and took it to him. Samuel felt loved, just like the people you made gifts for feel very loved. So when you are sitting around and thinking about someone you love very much, I hope you will remember this story of Hannah and the little coat she made for Samuel each year.

Closing Prayer

Thank you, God, for the people we love—moms and dads and grandparents and brothers and sisters and friends and teachers. These people are so special—thank you. Amen.

Suggestions for Delivery

This sermon will work especially well in a church with only a few children. I purposely kept the actual words spoken by the leader brief so that if it takes some time to decorate the hearts, the total sermon time will not be too long. However, if you have a very large group of children, or even a few children who are perfectionists, this sermon time might be too long. So an alternative would be to simply give each child a heart and skip the decorating part. Then ask them simply to take the heart and give it to someone. This will work fine.

Be prepared, though, for shy children to have a hard time giving their hearts away. They may be too shy to walk out into the congregation. Younger children might also have this problem. So be prepared to walk with these children and help them find a person to give their heart to, or you might even accept a heart yourself.

Samuel Is Called by God

Scriptural Base: *I Samuel 3:1-19*

Scriptural Summary

This is almost a comical story of the call of Samuel by God. Samuel is asleep and hears God call and keeps thinking that it is Eli calling him from the other room. Finally he understands that it is God, and God reveals a plan for Israel. Samuel is part of the plan.

Learning Objectives

By dividing the children into three groups and showing vividly the dynamics and humor of the story, the children will learn the story of Samuel's call by God. They should enjoy telling it, and it will show them that sometimes God speaks and we don't even recognize who it is.

The Sermon

Our scripture today is about Samuel, a great prophet of God. A prophet is a person who can hear God speak and then tells people what God is going to do. Well, this story is about the first time Samuel ever heard God speak to him. It is actually a pretty funny story as you will see. Now I am going to divide you into three groups. This group (a third of the children) is going to be God. This group (another third of the children) is going to be Samuel. And the last group (the last third of the children) is going to be Eli. Will you help me tell this story? (Let them respond.) When I point to your group and say something, I want you to repeat it. Here we go.

This is the story of the call of Samuel by God. Samuel was asleep one night and Eli was asleep in the next room. Samuel heard a voice say, (point to the God group) "Samuel, Samuel." (Let the God group repeat it.) So Samuel went to Eli's room and said (point to Samuel group), "Yes, Eli did you call?" (Let the Samuel group repeat it.) But Eli didn't call and said, (point to the Eli group) "No, I didn't call. Go back to bed." (Let the Eli group repeat it.)

But then it happened again. Samuel heard a voice, (point to the God group) "Samuel, Samuel." (Let the God group repeat.) And so Samuel went to Eli and said (point to the Samuel group), "Yes, did you call?" (Let the Samuel group repeat.) But Eli didn't call him, so he said, (point to the Eli group) "I didn't call you, go back to bed." (Let the Eli group repeat it.)

The same thing happened a third time. Samuel was asleep and heard God say, (point to the God group) "Samuel, Samuel." (Let the God group repeat it.) But Samuel didn't know who was calling so he went to Eli and said, (point to the Samuel group) "Eli, did you call me?" (Let the Samuel group repeat.) But this time Eli figured out that God must be calling and said, (point to the Eli group) "Go back to bed. It is God calling. The next time you hear it say, 'Here I am.'" (Let the Eli group repeat.)

So Samuel went to bed and once again heard God say, (point to God group) "Samuel, Samuel." (Let the God group repeat.) And this time Samuel said, (point to the Samuel group) "Yes, Lord, here I am." (Let the Samuel group repeat.)

Finally Samuel figured out that it wasn't Eli calling him, it was God. And God told Samuel that God had a plan and that Samuel would be part of it. And from then on, whenever Samuel heard God, he knew who was calling!

Closing Prayer

God, sometimes, just like Samuel, we don't hear what you want us to be or to do. Sometimes you call us by songs or music or stories, but we don't hear what you want us to hear. Please, keep calling us, keep pushing us to see you and understand what you would have us do. You kept calling Samuel; keep calling us. We pray in the name of Jesus. Amen.

Suggestions for Delivery

This sermon might seem confusing at first. Actually the story is somewhat confusing when first read. But once you are familiar with the story and the fact that God calls Samuel and Samuel keeps thinking that it is Eli calling, it is much simpler. I think this sermon will be quite effective if you tell the story as accurately as possible. It might be easier to memorize the basic flow of the story and have your hands free from the book while telling it.

Samuel Must Find a New King

Scriptural Base: *I Samuel 15:10-23*

Scriptural Summary

When first anointed king of Israel, Saul listened to all that God commanded him to do. But as time went on and Saul became more and more confident, he started doing things differently than God commanded. So God tells Samuel that he must tell Saul that he is no longer ruler and will not be the king of Israel. Samuel does not want to do this, but he does as the Lord tells him. Saul is very upset and begs Samuel to change his mind. But Samuel, who is only a messenger from God, cannot change God's decision. Saul is very upset and angry.

Learning Objectives

By using a visual image of Saul, the children will see how big-headed he got and how he stopped listening to God and started doing things his own way. The sermon stresses the need to do things God's way, rather than insisting on our own way.

Materials Needed

A balloon, a marker, and a pin.

The Sermon

Today I want to tell you a rather sad story about a man named Saul. Now pretend that this balloon is Saul. (Get out the balloon but do not inflate it yet.) Saul had been a regular kind of guy. Well, actually, he was handsome and strong, but he had a face just like everyone else had. (Draw eyes and nose and mouth while you talk.) He had eyes and a nose and ears and a mouth. But what made him very special was that he was chosen by God to be a king and lead the people of Israel. So I will draw a crown on him. (Draw the crown.) Every day, the Lord would tell Saul what to do that day and God filled his head with more and more wisdom. If he were to fight a battle, God would tell him how. (Blow up balloon a bit.) If he was to ration food, God would tell him how. (Blow up balloon a bit more.) If he was to do anything, God told him how to do it. (Blow up balloon a bit more.) This arrangement was great— until—Saul decided that he did not need God's advice. He knew how to do all those things, after all he was the king!

So Saul got very conceited and thought he knew more than God about how to run a country. Have you ever heard of a person's head swelling? Well that is just something we say when someone gets conceited. And boy did Saul's head swell! He got more and more conceited. (Blow up balloon more and more.)

God was not happy about this. So God sent Samuel to tell Saul about it, and Samuel knew it wasn't going to be any fun, but he did as God told him to. So Samuel went to Saul and said, "Saul, you are not listening to God and God is very angry. In fact God is not going to let you be ruler and will not let you continue as the king of Israel. You know all those dreams in your head, they are over."

Well poor Saul was very, very upset. Because he had been conceited and his head had swelled, he went right back to being a plain person again. (Let the air out of the balloon.) You know there are lots of laws and rules for us in the Bible. We read them and study them and try to follow them. And do you know why they are there? So that God can help us because we are awfully smart and we know a lot, but God knows much more than we do. Poor Saul (shake the deflated balloon) would have been much better off if he would have listened to God, and I think we will be much better off if we also listen to God!

Closing Prayer

God, we try to understand your rules and to follow them, but it is not always clear or an easy thing to do. Please help us to remember, though, that your ways are always the best for us. Help us to be open to your help and guidance. Amen.

Suggestions for Delivery

Children love balloons and so this story will probably keep their attention fairly easily if you keep the pace moving. The children may try to grab the balloon, so you should position yourself so that they cannot reach it. Remember to keep the air in the balloon until the end of the story. The purpose of the balloon is to make Saul's head get bigger and bigger.

David, a Very Good King

David Plays the Lyre for Saul

Scriptural Base: *I Samuel 16:14-23*

Scriptural Summary

Because of Saul's unwillingness to follow God's leadership, God has Samuel tell Saul that he will not be the king after all. Saul is so distressed over this news that he has spells of insanity where he is impossible to soothe. Saul's servants feel that some soothing music would help to calm Saul down, so they find David, a shepherd boy, who is quite skilled on the lyre. David comes and lives with Saul, and whenever Saul has a period of insanity, David's music brings him relief and comfort.

Learning Objectives

In this sermon the children will go through a series of solutions for Saul's problem. In doing so, they will discover that it was something as simple as music that helped him— and that was something a child could do. They will learn the story while at the same time be made aware of the strength and talent of a child. A less obvious lesson is that when faced with a problem, there is often more than one approach to solving it, and sometimes many tries must be made. The other less obvious lesson is that children can sometimes be as much help in solving problems as adults. There are so few stories of children as helpers in the Bible, this story will speak strongly to the children.

63

Materials Needed

A pretend bottle of medicine, some baby oil marked "Holy Oil," a pair of tennis shoes, an instrument of some kind, either a real one or a toy will work fine.

The Sermon

Today I want to tell you a story about a man named Saul who had a very big problem. Then I want you to help me solve his problem, all right? Saul had been promised by God that he would someday be a great king but he did not do the things God told him to do, so God decided that someone else should be the king. How do you think poor old Saul felt when he found out that someone else would get to be king? (Give the children time to respond. They will say things like: sad, angry, disappointed.) Yes, Saul felt all of those things. He was really, really, really upset! He was so upset he couldn't think of anything else. In fact he got so upset that at times he would go crazy and get into a huge rage and no one could calm him down.

Well, Saul's servants saw how Saul was acting and so they knew they had to help him. Now there were several things that they might have done. The first thing was that they might have taken him to the doctor and gotten some medicine for Saul. (Show the children the medicine bottle and place it where they can see it.) What do you think about that idea? (Give them a chance to respond.) Yes, I think calling a doctor would be a good idea. After all, doctors are grown ups and they have medicine and they are very smart. OK, so the doctor is our first option.

The second idea they might have had was to call a minister to come and pray for Saul. And in those days, ministers often used holy oil to help people while they prayed. So I'll put the bottle of holy oil here to remind us of the minister. (Place the oil beside the medicine bottle.) What do you think of this idea? (Give the children time to respond.) Yes I think that would be a nice idea. After all, ministers are adults and very smart and very holy. OK, so the second option would be to call a minister. We have two options so far, a doctor or a minister.

The third idea the servants might have considered was to help Saul get more exercise. So they might have called an aerobics teacher. I'll put these tennis shoes here to remind us of the aerobics teacher. (Place the tennis shoes next to the other objects.) What do you think of 'his idea? (Give the children time to respond.) I think the aerobics teacher would be a pretty good idea. After all, he or she would be an adult and would know how to help Saul get more exercise. Maybe that would help. OK, now we have three choices. They could call the doctor, an adult who could give Saul some medicine, they could call a minister who is an adult and could pray for Saul, or they could call an aerobics teacher and help Saul get more exercise.

Now they might have one more idea. They could find a child who played an instrument and have the child play for Saul to see if music could calm him down. I'll put this musical instrument here to remind us of the child who could play music. (Place the instrument next to the other objects.) What do you think of this idea? (Give the children time to respond. Some will like the idea, others will not.) Personally, I think this might be all right, but do you think a child could actually help? Or do we need to use these adults like the doctor, or minister, or aerobics teacher? (Again give them a chance to respond.)

I told you I wanted you to help me solve Saul's problem. We have four options, the doctor, the minister, the aerobics teacher, and the child with a musical instrument. Which option do you think will work for Saul? (Give several children a chance to respond and tell why they chose the option they did.)

The Bible tells us that Saul went crazy because he couldn't be king and his servants had to help him. So (pause) they didn't call the adult doctor, (put the medicine away) and . . . (pause) they didn't call the adult minister, (put the Bible away) and (pause) they didn't call the adult aerobics teacher. The servants called (pause and hold up the instrument) the child! And guess what? It worked. A child who played an instrument called a lyre, which is sort of like a harp, came to Saul, and whenever Saul had his spells of craziness and couldn't be calmed down, this child would play music and calm him down. The child's name was David.

Can you believe it? All those adults might have helped, but it was a child who did. Sometimes children can be a big help to those around them. I think children are very special people!

Closing Prayer

God, these children have come to church today to worship and praise you. Help them to realize that they are each very special to you and to me and to their family and friends. I pray that each day they are reminded of how special they are and how much help they can be to others. I pray in the name of your son, Jesus who loved children very much. Amen.

Suggestions for Delivery

This sermon shows in a dramatic way that children are important and special. Often they feel unimportant and powerless in a world of adults. So when delivering this sermon, you must stress the word "adult" whenever it appears.

The more you stress "adult" the more contrast there will be between the adult's ability to help others and the child's. Then, when it is revealed that a child turned out to be the greatest help, the children will be surprised, and my guess is that they will be delighted.

Also at the end of the sermon, when you are eliminating the objects, be very playful and stretch it out. The pauses are there to help create a sense of drama. The children will be eager to know who helped Saul and will enjoy the drama of finding out at last.

David Fights Goliath

Scriptural Base: *I Samuel 17:12-54*

Scriptural Summary

Saul's army comes face to face with the Philistines and Goliath, who is a giant, issues a challenge to Saul's army. He tells them to choose one man to fight him. If Goliath wins, the Israelites will be the slaves of the Philistines but if Goliath loses, the Philistines will be the slaves of the Israelites. All the men of Saul's army were afraid and no one wanted to face the giant. David, a small shepherd boy, hears the challenge and decides to fight Goliath. At first Saul refuses, but he eventually lets David fight. David faces Goliath and Goliath tries to intimidate David, but David will not back down. He takes a stone and sling shot, hits Goliath with it, and kills him. He then cuts off Goliath's head and there is great rejoicing.

Learning Objectives

Children today are very aware of the world around them, both the good things and the frightening things. In this story David, a boy, is able to face a big problem, the giant, because he never doubted that God was with him. This sermon attempts to teach children this story of faith and courage while at the same time helping them identify their own fears and assure them that God is with them as they face their problems, the same way God was with David so long ago.

Materials Needed

Several large boxes and a marker.

The Sermon

There is a very exciting story in the Bible about a boy who fought a huge giant. I'll bet some of you know this story already, but I want to tell it to you again. There was a man named Saul who had an army and was going to fight the mean Philistines. Now the Philistines were very mean and the army was afraid of them. One of the Philistines was especially mean. His name was Goliath, and he was a giant. One day Goliath shouted over to the army of Saul and said, "I'll make a deal. Instead of having a big war, choose one of your men to fight me. Then if I win, you have to do as we say, and if he wins, we Philistines will do as you say." It sounded OK except no one was brave enough to fight Goliath.

A boy named David was visiting the camp one day and he heard about Goliath. He was a shepherd boy and had killed a lion before when he was protecting the sheep. He wasn't afraid of Goliath.

At first Saul didn't want David to fight, but he had no choice—David was the only one who was brave enough to try. So he took a sling shot and five stones and he walked right up to Goliath. He threw a stone into the middle of his head and he killed the giant. Do you know why David was so brave? (Give the children time to respond.) Because he had a very strong faith in God and knew that no matter how afraid he was, God would be there to help him and protect him. So David was able to face Goliath because he believed in God and depended on God to help him.

I know that kids today don't have to be afraid of giants like Goliath, but I'll bet there are other things that you are afraid of—things that you might be worried about or scared of in our world.

So I am going to build a big giant of scary things out of these boxes. I will write one scary thing on each of these

69

boxes, and I need you to help me by telling me things that you are afraid of. (Give the children time to tell you things they are afraid of. Write one fear on each box and stack them up on top of each other.) We have made a pretty scary giant here. It is made of (read each fear out loud again). Sometimes things we are afraid of seem very big and overwhelming, like this giant. Do you think David felt scared and overwhelmed when he saw Goliath? (Give them time to respond.) Remember that David felt strong and confident because he knew that God would be right beside him when he faced this giant. This giant we have made is pretty scary, too. Do you think God will be with us when we have to face these things? (Let the children respond.) I do too. God is always with us, no matter what we have to deal with or face. And with God beside us, even the scariest giant isn't so scary. (Knock the boxes over.)

Closing Prayer

God, I wish that life wasn't full of things that make us afraid or unsure. But since it is, it is good to know that you will always be with us and help us face the things we don't want to face. In times when we are unsure or afraid, please be with us as you were with David when he fought Goliath. All power and glory are yours, now and always. Amen.

Suggestions for Delivery

This sermon begins with the story of David and Goliath. I have written it out in narrative form but feel free to tell it in any form you feel comfortable with and don't hesitate to elaborate. It should be told with enthusiasm to keep the children's attention. But it is an exciting story and one that children like, so it will keep their attention easily.

The boxes are used to make a huge giant by stacking them on top of each other. You must be able to stack the boxes so they don't fall over before you knock them over. This will require a bit of practice. It is also fine to have another adult there to steady the stack. The larger the boxes, the taller the giant will be and the more overwhelming the giant is, the more impressive the lesson will be.

At the end when you knock the boxes over there might be laughing or cheering. That is fine and, in fact, the children will be happy that their fears are knocked over so it would be natural for them to respond.

Jonathan, David's Best Friend

Scriptural Base: *I Samuel 19:1-7*

Scriptural Summary

Jonathan was the son of Saul. Saul was supposed to be the anointed king but had the right taken from him because of disobedience to God. He is very jealous of David and his bravery against Goliath. Jonathan, who is David's best friend, comes to David's defense and Saul promises not to harm David. However, Saul's jealousy continues to grow in later chapters and Jonathan again helps David.

Learning Objectives

This sermon attempts to teach the children the name of Jonathan who was David's true friend for life, while at the same time teaching them the story of friendship the two shared. This is one of the few stories in the Bible of close friends whose friendship lasts as long as this one does. It is an important story for the children to learn.

Materials Needed

Eight sheets of paper with one large letter on one side and the other side blank. The papers when put together will spell "Jonathan."

The Sermon

I think that friends are one of the most important things in our life. Do you have any friends? What are some of your friends names? (Let the children shout out names of friends.) I have a lot of friends too. Do you have a best friend? (Give them time to respond.)

Our Bible story today is about a boy named David who had a best friend when he was a child and kept that friend for his whole life. I need eight helpers. (Choose eight children and line them up facing the congregation. Give them each a card in the proper order and tell them not to show their letter until you tell them to turn it over.)

As I tell you stories about David and his friend, I will have the helpers turn their paper over and a letter will show. Then at the end we will find out what the name of David's best friend was.

David was a brave child who fought and killed a very mean giant and so lots of people were jealous of David, especially David's friend's father, Saul. But David's friend was never jealous of David. The word jealous begins with a "J" and that is the first letter of David's friend's name. (Have the first child show the "J.")

David's friend was also never ashamed of being friends with David; he openly told others how much he liked David. Openly begins with "O" the second letter in the friend's name. (Have the second child show the "O.")

And the friend really cared about David and never purposely hurt him by something he did or said. Never begins with "N," the third letter in the friend's name. (Have the third child show the "N.")

The friend also always wanted the best for David. Always begins with an "A" and that is the next letter in the friend's name. (Have the next child show the "A.")

This friend always told David the truth. If he made a promise, he kept it! Truth begins with a "T" and that is our next letter. (Have the child holding "T" turn it over.)

Now this friend's father was very, very jealous of David and even wanted to kill him. David's friend helped him to hide from his father, Saul, until he was safe. "Helped" begins with "H" and so that is our next letter. (Have the child turn the "H" over.)

When Saul would talk meanly about David, his friend would always stand up for David and defend him. Always begins with "A" and it is the next letter. (Have the child holding the "A" turn it over.)

And last but not least, David's friend never stopped being David's friend. Never begins with "N" and it is the last letter of David's friend's name. Why don't you read his name with me. (Let them read the name.) Yes, Jonathan was a good friend, the best friend that David ever had. Jonathan was never jealous of David, openly liked David, never purposely hurt David, always wanted the best for David, told David the truth, helped David in times of trouble, always stood up for David and defended him, and never stopped being his friend. Jonathan was a good friend to David. Hey, I was just thinking, if we wanted to be a good friend to someone, we could do these things too. We could stop being jealous of them, openly like them and not care about what others thought, never purposely hurt them, always want the best for them, tell them the truth, help them in times of trouble, always stand up for them when others say mean things, and never stop being their friend. David was lucky to have a friend like Jonathan, and I know that someone out there is very lucky to have a best friend like you!

Closing Prayer

God, we thank you for all of our friends and pray that you help us to be a good friend to them as well. We also thank you for being our friend who is always beside us and always there to help us and care for us. We pray in the name of your son who was such a good friend to so many people. Amen.

Suggestions for Delivery

The children, especially the ones who are learning to read, will really enjoy this sermon as they try to figure out the name of David's friend. Try to have them figure it out silently and not spoil it for the others. Then have them all read it at the end.

Finding eight children could be hard if you are with a small congregation. I suggest either asking adults to hold the cards and let the children read them or having four children each hold two cards. Then the congregation could be asked to read the name out loud. The children enjoy knowing that the adults are learning with them and so this would work out fine.

It is obvious but worth mentioning that the letters printed on the cards should be large enough and bold enough to be read by the entire congregation.

Wise Abigail Meets David

Scriptural Base: *I Samuel 25:3-43*

Scriptural Summary

On a feast day, David sends his men to the home of a man named Nabal and asks if they might celebrate with him. He is described as a cold, mean person, and he refuses David. When Nabal's wife, Abigail, hears of David's request, she takes two hundred loaves of bread, wine, and sheep and gives them to David and asks him to spare the life of her husband. David agrees and so decides not to attack Nabal and his men because of her generosity. The next day Abigail tells her husband what she has done, and he is so angry that he dies. David then marries Abigail.

Learning Objectives

Clearly the lesson in this story is that generosity and kindness are better than a hard heart. Through role playing situations familiar to the children, they will learn about what generosity means and identify with Abigail who showed generosity to David.

Materials Needed

None

The Sermon

Today I want to tell you a story about a man named David. David was a person who was blessed by God and always did as God told him. The story is found in the book of First Samuel in the Bible. One day David and his army were traveling to a place called Paran and on their way they remembered it was a holiday. Well, they had no place to celebrate, so David sent his men to a man named Nabal to ask if they might celebrate the holiday with him. But Nabal was a mean man and would not share his food with them. David was very angry and was going to attack Nabal and his army and fight them.

Luckily, Nabal had a nice wife named Abigail who was generous, not greedy like Nabal. She heard that David wanted to celebrate the holiday with them and so she took two hundred loaves of bread, some wine, and some sheep to David so that he and his men could celebrate. She then begged David not to attack her husband Nabal and his men. Because she was so generous, David agreed not to attack and thanked her for all she had done.

The two people in this story are very different. Nabal was selfish and would not share, but Abigail was generous and gladly shared what she had. You know, we all have times when we are expected to share what we have with others. And we can react in two ways, like Nabal—greedy and refusing to share—or like Abigail—generous and willing to share.

I am going to tell you some different situations, and I want you to tell me which way Nabal would respond to it, and which way Abigail would respond. Are you ready? OK, here is the first situation. After school two friends walk to the candy store to buy some candy. But when they get there, one of them discovers that she has lost her money. The friend without money turns to the other and says, "If you will buy me some candy today, I will buy you some candy tomorrow." Now, if the other friend was Nabal, what would he or she say? (Give the children time to respond.) You are right. Nabal would say, "Tough luck. I am not going to help you out." If the other friend was Abigail, what do you think she would say? (Give the children time to respond.) You are right. Abigail would probably say, "That is fine. I will gladly share with you and you can share with me tomorrow." Abigail is very generous and God wants us to be generous toward others.

Let's try another one. Let's imagine that someone is walking down the street and he is in a hurry to get to baseball practice. He sees a little .ild crying and looking at a tree. He stops to ask what is wrong, and the little girl says that her cat is in the tree and can't get down. She is very upset. Now if the boy on his way to baseball was Nabal, what would he do? (Give the children time to respond.) You are right. He would probably say, "Hey, sorry, I don't have time to help you. I have to go to baseball practice." But what if the person was Abigail? What would she do then? (Give the children time to respond.) You are right again! Abigail would probably help and then explain to the coach why she was late to practice. Abigail would act generously and that is what God wants us to do.

Let's do one more. Imagine that it is Christmas morning and a family is just getting ready to open their gifts from Santa when they hear a knock on the door. On the porch is a family whose home had just burned down early that morning. They have no Christmas dinner, no presents from Santa, and no place to spend Christmas. The family knows that if they let this other family in they will have to share dinner with them and even their Santa toys. If this family was Nabal, what would they do? (Give the children time to respond.) You are very good at this. Nabal would turn the family away. What about Abigail? (Give the children time to respond.) Yes, Abigail would help the family and share Christmas with them. Abigail is generous and that is the way God wants us to be.

You will have many times when someone comes to you and asks you for help. And when they do, I hope you will remember this story of Nabal and Abigail, and I hope you will act as Abigail did. It isn't always easy, but being generous is the way God wants us to be.

Closing Prayer

God, sometimes people ask us for help when we don't want to help, when we are too busy or in a hurry and it would be easy for us to say, "No, go away." But at those times, help us to pause and remember the story of Abigail and her generosity to David and help us to respond as she did so long ago. We pray in the name of your son, who was never too busy to stop and help those who asked. Amen.

Suggestions for Delivery

Children love to express their opinions, especially when they will be listened to, so this sermon should capture and keep their attention. Be sure to let them respond to the questions asked, but don't spend too long on each scenario or they will get bored and stop listening. There is a fine line between hearing their answers and losing their focus.

The story at the beginning of the sermon is the basis for the entire sermon so it should be told with excitement and interest.

David Becomes King!

Scriptural Summary

After the death of Saul, David continues in the favor of the Lord and is finally anointed king over Israel. He prays to God, praising God for all the good works God has done through him. He feels unworthy to be king. He then asks God to bless him and to let him continue being a servant to God all the days of his life.

Learning Objectives

This sermon teaches the children that David was a good king because he relied on God for help and guidance and direction, which is evidenced by his prayer. It will stress that no matter what our job in life might be, asking God to help us is a good thing to do.

Materials Needed

A paper crown.

The Sermon

Many of you have heard stories about David when he was a little boy. David was a shepherd boy who played a lyre. When King Saul was very ill, David would play music and calm him down. Then when David heard of a very mean giant who was going to fight Saul's army, David went face to fight with him and killed him with one stone in a sling shot. David was a boy who had a lot of faith in God and always believed that God was with him to help him. As David grew older, he stayed faithful to God. So when David became a man, God rewarded him for his faithfulness and made him the King of Israel. Kings in Bible times were like kings today. They had power and money and could have anything they wanted!

What if you were made a king? What would you want more than anything else? I am going to have each of you become king. After I place the crown on you, I want you to tell us what you want. (Give each child a chance to tell what they want.) Those were good ideas. I want some of those things too. David probably wanted lots of things when he was king also. Perhaps he wanted a palace, a swimming pool, and good things to eat like lots of candy, and a horse, and twenty dogs. I'll bet he wanted a lot of things. But do you know what he wanted more than anything? (Give the children time to guess.)

In the Second Book of Samuel, David says a beautiful prayer to God. In the prayer he asks God for the thing he wants the most. David wanted more than anything to be blessed by God and to always follow God and do whatever God wanted him to. David wanted more than anything for God to stay close beside him.

Probably none of us will become kings when we grow up. We will be teachers and ministers and doctors and nurses and scientists and moms and dads. But whatever we become, I hope we remember this story of David, the king who could have had anything he wanted but who asked only to always stay close to God. Whatever you become in your life, I hope you stay close to God. David did stay close to God when he became the king and he was a great one. When you stay close to God, whatever you do, you do it better!

81

Closing Prayer

God, these children have their whole lives in front of them. They will be students in school, take music lessons, and play games. Then they will grow into teenagers, and then into adults. At every step of their lives, remind them that you are close to them and guiding them. Whatever happens to them as they grow, they can always depend on you! Thank you for always being close to us. Amen.

Suggestions for Delivery

The children will most likely enjoy putting on the crown and pretending to be a king. If you have too many children to have each one be king, select several and let them do it. However it is better if each child can have a turn because it starts their thinking process and gets them involved. If you do select children, choose both boys and girls. This is pretend, and in pretend, girls can be kings as well as boys.

The purpose of having the children ask for something is to help show the humanness of David. He too wanted material things. But the difference between him and other kings was his desire to be close to God. So be careful not to make fun of the children's requests.

Also be prepared for children who want things like "world peace" and "happiness." These things are great and will not effect the direction of the sermon. If the children say things like that, after you tell them what David wanted you might want to say something like, "And when we ask God to help us maybe some of the things you asked for, like world peace, could really happen."

David Dies and Solomon Becomes King

Scriptural Base: *I Kings 2:1-12*

Scriptural Summary

When David was about to die, he called his son Solomon to his side and blessed him and gave instructions for how to be a wise king. David tells his son to keep the laws of God and to walk the path that God would have him walk and his kingdom will thrive. Then David dies a peaceful death and Solomon takes over as king.

Learning Objectives

This passage would be wise council for any parent to give to their child. In this sermon I hope that the children really listen to what David has to say. By beginning to memorize it with motions, perhaps it will be ingrained in their memories.

Materials Needed

None

The Sermon

King David was a very wise king and a very good king because he always tried to do whatever God asked him to and to follow God closely. Today I want to tell you about his death. Now this isn't really a sad story because even though David died, his kingdom was able to go on because he had a son named Solomon who became king and also did a great job as king. He did such a great job because he listened to what his father, King David, said to him as he was dying.

King David called his son Solomon to him and said, "Son, if you want to be a great king, this is what you should do. Be strong, be courageous, and do as God would have you do. Walk in God's ways, keep God's laws, and you will prosper in all you do."

Solomon listened to his father and did the things he said and turned out to be a great king. But I don't think that this advice is just for kings. I think we should all try to live this way and we would prosper in all we do as well. I want you to remember this advice as you grow, so let's say it together. I will say a line and do a motion, and then I want you to repeat the line and do the motion.

To excel and do well in life this is what we should do:
Be strong (make a muscle)
(*children repeat*)
Be courageous (place your fist on your heart)
(*children repeat*)
And do as God would have you do. (place hands as if praying and point towards the sky)
(*children repeat*)
Walk in God's ways. (walk in place)
(*children repeat*)
Keep God's laws (pound hand with fist as if a gavel in a court)
(*children repeat*)
As it was written by Moses (make hands as if holding a book)
(*children repeat*)
And you will prosper in all you do. (make broad sweeping motion with both hands)
(*children repeat*)

You know, I think this is very good advice. It was good advice to Solomon and it is good advice to us.

Closing Prayer

God, help us to be strong and courageous and to always walk in your ways. Help us to follow the advice of David and be wise and good just as both David and Solomon were. We pray in the name of your son who was the wisest and best of all. Amen.

Suggestions for Delivery

In order to help the children better understand the text, I haxve simplified it. If that bothers you, feel free to use the Bible text (1 Kings 2:1-4) and use the same motions.

Children like to repeat things and do motions so they should enjoy this sermon. If you have time, let them repeat the entire thing more than once. The congregation will enjoy hearing and seeing it more than once and the more the children say it, the better they will remember it. Children are amazing at memorizing. Many of them will be able to learn this passage with one or two repetitions.

Joshua, a Warrior for God

The Promise of the Promised Land

Scriptural Base: *Joshua 1:1-18*

Scriptural Summary

After the death of Moses, God tells Joshua that the time is near to cross into the promised land. But to do so, the people must listen carefully and do as God tells them. Joshua gives them their orders, and the people respond favorably. They trust in Joshua's leadership and believe in him.

Learning Objectives

By playing a game similar to follow the leader, the children will see that Joshua was a good leader and that the people chose to follow him. This sermon attempts to impress upon the children what a good leader Joshua was so that when they hear the name Joshua they will equate it with leader and follower of God.

Materials Needed

None

The Sermon

Today I want to tell you a story about the people of Israel. These poor people had been taken prisoners and made slaves by the Pharaoh in Egypt for many, many years.

They prayed to God to help them and so God sent Moses to free them. Well they were freed and then had to live for many, many years in the wilderness. It was a hard time for them and they got tired and doubted if God was really with them many times. Then their leader Moses died and they became afraid. That is where our Scripture lesson for today begins. Joshua becomes the leader of the people, and finally the time comes for the people to enter the promised land and not have life so hard. But God tells Joshua that the people must do as God tells them and must trust and follow Joshua very closely.

It was sort of like playing follow the leader. Whatever Joshua did, the people had to do. So I thought that we could play follow the leader while I tell you what Joshua told the people.
Whatever I say or do, you must do.

This is the word of God. (point to the sky)
(*children repeat*)
You must be strong and courageous. (make a muscle)
(*children repeat*)
You must do as Moses told you. (shake finger as if scolding)
(*children repeat*)
You must keep the laws close by. (hold hands as if reading a book)
(*children repeat*)
You must pray (fold hands as if praying)
(*children repeat*)
And you must think about God's words. (point to forehead)
(*children repeat*)
And you must listen to Joshua (point to ears)
(*children repeat*)
And do whatever Joshua says. (shake finger as if scolding)
(*children repeat*)

Wow, you played follow the leader so well! You did whatever I did, and do you know what? The people of Israel played follow the leader well also. They did exactly what Joshua told them to do, and since Joshua only told them what God told him, the people of Israel finally got to cross into the promised land. And do you know that if they had chosen not to follow Joshua, they wouldn't have gotten to do it.

We read the Bible and try to do what God tells us to do. That is sort of like playing follow the leader with God, isn't it?

Closing Prayer

God, we read your holy words and we learn in church and Sunday school and at home about your laws. Help us to follow your ways as closely as the people of Israel followed Joshua and as closely as Joshua followed you. It isn't always clear or easy, but we are trying. And remind us when we mess up and don't follow you that your forgiveness is always there for us. Amen.

Suggestions for Delivery

The children will like playing this game of follow the leader but remember to keep the pace moving so that the young ones will stay interested. Don't worry about the children who make mistakes and don't point it out. The point of the sermon is how well the people of Israel followed Joshua, not how they had made mistakes earlier.

Rahab Helps Joshua's Men

Scriptural Base: *Joshua 2:1-24*

Scriptural Summary

Joshua sends two of his men to spy on Jericho so they can decide how to attack it and claim the land which God had given them. The two men stay at the home of Rahab, a prostitute. The king of Jericho learns that the spies are there and goes to Rahab and asks her to bring them out. Rahab knows that they are men of God, so she hides them and then helps them escape. She asks them to spare her and her family when Jericho is attacked. They tell her to tie a red ribbon on her door, and they will not hurt anyone in her home. They return to Joshua and tell him the story of a woman who saw that they were men of God.

Learning Objectives

Rahab was a very faith-filled person to recognize that the spies were sent by God. By using pictures of people and having the children try to guess what they do, this sermon tries to impress upon them that sometimes we see with more than our eyes, we feel with our faith.

Materials Needed

A picture of Jesus and pictures of several other people (they can be photos or cut from magazines).

The Sermon

(Hold up the picture of Jesus) Do you know who this is? (Give the children time to respond.) Yes, it is Jesus. But how did you know? (Let them respond.) Do you know there are people who never heard about Jesus and never saw any pictures of him and if they saw this picture, they wouldn't know who it was?

It would be like me showing you pictures of people you never saw and asking you what they did for a living. Here, let me show you. I have several pictures of people here and I am going to show them to you. Then I want you to tell me what these people do for a living—are they doctors or teachers or what? (Show the pictures. The children will not be able to tell you what they do and will probably laugh or giggle.) What is the matter? Why can't you tell me who these people are? (Let the children respond.)

I know it is hard, in fact, it is impossible. Our story today is about a woman named Rahab who lived in Jericho. Two men she had not seen before came to her hotel to stay. They were spies sent by Joshua and God to spy on Jericho. The king of the city heard that the spies were there and so he went to Rahab and told her to bring them to him. But Rahab didn't. She had never seen these men before and yet something told her that they were men of God and that she should hide them. You had never seen the people's pictures that I showed you, and so you couldn't tell anything about them. How do you think Rahab knew that these men were men of God? (Let the children theorize.) Well, I am not sure but I think that Rahab believed in God and it was her faith that told her these were good men and men sent by God.

So Rahab knew the men were sent by God and helped them escape. Then she asked them if, since she had helped them, they would not hurt her and her family when they attacked Jericho in a battle. They told her to place a red ribbon on her door and everyone inside would be safe.

Then the men went back to Joshua and told them about a woman who had never seen them before, but by her faith knew that God had sent them. How lucky they were to find Rahab, a woman with a lot of faith.

Closing Prayer

Dear God, as we hear stories about faith, help us to know that as we grow our faith will grow as well. We pray that sometime our faith might be as strong and as developed as Rahab's faith was. Please guide us and help us to feel your presence as we grow both physically and spiritually.

Suggestions for Delivery

The picture of Jesus that is shown to the children should be one that will be easily identified. It should be large enough so that others can see it as well. The pictures of strangers that you show should also be large enough for the entire group of children to see at once. If the pictures have to be passed around it will take too much time and the children will turn their attention away.

Joshua Fights at Jericho

Scriptural Base: *Joshua 6:1-21*

Scriptural Summary

God decided that the time had come for Joshua to overtake the city of Jericho since it rightfully belonged to the Israelites. So God gave Joshua a plan. For six days Joshua and his army were to march around the city one time each day. Then on the seventh day, they were to walk around the city seven times with the priests blowing their trumpets. The seventh time around, the soldiers were to make a loud cry and the city walls would fall. Joshua and his army did as God commanded and the city of Jericho was reclaimed.

Learning Objectives

This story is one that every child should have stored away in his or her memories. The major learning objective is to teach them the story using dramatics as the approach. A secondary lesson is that God is wise and strong. We benefit from God's wisdom only if we do as God wants us to.

Materials Needed

A set of blocks.

The Sermon

I have a set of blocks here. Do you like to play with blocks? What kinds of things do you like to make out of blocks? (Give the children time to respond.) Today I want to tell you a story about a man named Joshua who was sent by God to reclaim a city that belonged to the people of Israel. The city was named Jericho. It was a large city and it was hard to capture because it had a huge wall around it.

I want to build the city of Jericho. Would you help me? Let's make the inside of Jericho first. Let's make some houses and buildings. (Give the children time to build it.) That looks great. Now, do you remember what Jericho had all around it? A wall. Let's build a wall around Jericho. (Let the children make a wall.) That looks so good.

Now we are ready to learn the story about Jericho. I need someone to pretend to be Joshua. (Select one child.) Joshua, God has given you a plan to capture this city. You and your army are to walk around the city one time each day for six days. Then, on the seventh day, you are to walk around it seven times and blow your trumpets. After the seventh time you are all to shout. How does the plan sound? (Let Joshua respond.)

The rest of you are Joshua's army. So it is the first day. Joshua lead your people around this city once. (Let them circle the city.) Now it is day three. (Joshua will lead them around the city.) It is day five. (Repeat the circling.) Now it is day seven. Do you remember what you have to do on day seven? (Let the children respond.) On the seventh day, you have to circle the city seven times blowing your trumpets. On the seventh time around, you have to shout really loud. OK, Joshua, lead them. (They circle seven times. It is a good idea to help them by counting aloud each time they make a circle.) Now, you've circled seven times: Shout! Really shout, let me hear you. (Let them shout.)

Well the soldiers did exactly what God said to do and guess what? The walls of Jericho came tumbling down (knock over the blocks) and the army could walk right in and capture it.

I don't know about you but that plan really didn't sound very good to me. I mean, who would ever think it would work? It just shows us that God is definitely wiser than we are, and so it is always good to listen to God's plans for our lives and do as God says. I am surely glad that Joshua and his army listened to God, aren't you?

Closing Prayer

Dear God, Sometimes we do not understand why you have made some of your laws and rules for us to follow. But help us to remember that you are wise. We can trust and follow you knowing that your plan is always the best one for our lives. We pray in the name of your son who followed your plans his entire life. Amen.

Suggestions for Delivery

This sermon will work well if it is staged properly. For example, the children need to be shown where to walk and where to stand after they circle the city. I suggest taking a moment and explaining to them where and when to walk. Otherwise they might start pushing and fall into the city.

This is a fun sermon. It should be fun for the children, so laughing is all right. The point will be made when they see the walls crumble, whether or not they have been concentrating on the story.

If you have a large group and limited space, you may need to select a few children to act out the drama.

Scripture Index